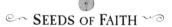

SEEDS of FAITH

Love

SEEDS OF FAITH

Love

Words of Faith from
NORMAN VINCENT PEALE

Ideals Publications · Nashville, Tennessee

ISBN 0-8249-4634-0

Published by Ideals Publications, a division of Guideposts
535 Metroplex Drive, Suite 250, Nashville, Tennessee 37211
www.idealsbooks.com

Editor, Peggy Schaefer
Designer, Marisa Calvin
Cover photograph: D. Hurst/Alamy Images

Printed and bound in Mexico by RR Donnelley
10 9 8 7 6 5 4 3 2 1

ACKNOWLEDGMENTS
The material by Norman Vincent Peale contained in this book is used
by permission of Guideposts, Carmel, New York.

All Scripture quotations, unless otherwise noted, are taken from
The King James Version of the Bible.

Scripture quotations marked (RSV) are taken from the Revised
Standard Version of the Bible. Copyright © 1946, 1952, 1971 by
Division of Christian Education of the National Council of Churches of
Christ in the U.S.A. Used by permission. All rights reserved.

Scripture quotations marked (GNT) are taken from the Good News
Bible, Second Edition, Today's English Version, Copyright © 1992 by
American Bible Society. Used by permission. All rights reserved.

The most curative thought in the world
is the thought of love.

—Norman Vincent Peale

FOREWORD

Throughout his long career, my father, Norman Vincent Peale, valued no message more than that of the importance of faith in each of our lives. In fact, before the title was finalized, *The Power of Positive Thinking* was called *The Power of Faith*. It was that important to him.

Growing up in the Midwest at the beginning of the twentieth century, Dad learned about faith at his parents' knees and in the pews of small-town churches. Faith in God, country, and fellow man, and the saving message of Jesus Christ filled his youthful days. He learned oratorical skills by listening to the great preachers of the day,

who went from town to town, bringing countless people to faith. He became filled with faith messages, and they never left him.

When the personal call came for him to enter the ministry, Dad was well equipped with deep faith, a gift for communicating, and a love of people. His writings were full of anecdotes of the faith journeys of countless people he met along the way. By their examples, he was able to lead others to a life of faith. His was a great calling, and I think we can all agree that he succeeded.

As you read, I hope you enjoy the messages in this book and that it brings deeper faith into your life.

—*Elizabeth Peale Allen*

This is my commandment, *That ye* **love** one another, as I have **loved** you.

—John 15:12

*I*f it were possible to sum up the teachings of Christianity in one word, that word would be *love*. "A new commandment I give unto you," said Jesus to His disciples at the Last Supper, "That ye love one another; as I have loved you, that ye also love one another," (John 13:34).

Christianity, in its essence, in the simple teach-

ings of Jesus, is a religion of love. And this emphasis on love is not only for the purpose of making the earth a better world, although a better world will come when we truly love one another. The Gospel stresses love because a person needs love in his heart, both for himself and for other people, to live creatively and successfully.

Smiley Blanton, a great psychiatrist, teacher, and lover of humanity, wrote:

> Either you love or you will perish. To say that one will perish without love does not mean that everyone without adequate love dies. Many do, for without love the will to

live is often impaired to such an extent that a person's resistance is critically lowered and death follows. But most of the time, lack of love makes people depressed, anxious, and without zest for life. They remain lonely and unhappy, without friends or work they care for, their life a barren treadmill, stripped of all creative action and joy.

Love or perish! No wonder Jesus makes love central to His whole teaching! If you are going to live creatively, you must learn to love.

Now, to avoid any misunderstandings when talking about love, let's first define it.

The kind of love I am talking about is not the

type that is dished up in soap operas or in the movies. Neither is it the kind that revolves around romantic relationships. Romantic love has its place in life, but it doesn't need any extra emphasis. It gets along pretty well on its own! The kind of love I mean is a deep feeling for others—for people in general—that is often hard to express. If you are seeking understanding and help from someone, you can experience this feeling in a smile, a handshake, a pat on the shoulder or on the back. These gestures transmit a feeling that cannot easily be put into words.

Love comes first in creative living, and to have it,

you must love yourself. This is primary. Do you truly love yourself?

"Oh," you say, "that's easy. I sure do like myself. I am proud of myself."

But wait a minute. That isn't love. That is egotism. True love of yourself is having a deep, joyous respect for yourself, being mindful of your God-given abilities and capabilities, and using them to the fullest extent possible.

The Gospel indicates that, without this wholesome loving respect for yourself, you cannot really love anyone else. It tells us, "Thou shalt love thy neighbour as thyself" (Matthew 19:19). This implies

We grow by love
. . . others are our nutriment.

WILLIAM ELLERY CHANNING

that if you don't love yourself, you won't love your neighbor. But if you do love and respect yourself as a child of God, then you can likewise love and respect another person as a child of God.

Every human being has a story. All you have to do is show people you like them, and presently they will start talking. I was asked one day, "Where do you get all your tales about people?" The answer is, from people. People are lovable and delightful.

If you want people to like you, each morning say, "Lord, help me to love everyone I see today: help me at least to like them. Help me to see the good in them." Get to loving people and your whole personality will change, and love will come back to you.

If you want to love yourself, you need to develop a healthy spiritual self-esteem, so by all means seek to have it. Pray about it; read the Bible; get closer to God. You will learn to love yourself as you become increasingly aware of God's everlasting, unremitting, constant love for you.

One of the greatest statements ever made is this: "For God so loved the world, that he gave his only begotten Son, that whosoever believeth in him should not perish, but have everlasting life" (John 3:16). If you were called upon to demonstrate love, what greater example could you give than this? It's the most poignant gift of love ever known in all the history of mankind.

There is no circumstance in your life where God will not stand with you and help you. He understands all your troubles, all your frustrations and disappointments. He understands your many weaknesses. He loves you.

He is a loving God. He loves you more dearly than your mother loves you, or your father, or your spouse. You are His child. So just get to know Him and trust His love. Then you will have that wholesome esteem for your own self that leads to having respect and love for all people.

Once you've learned to trust God in all things, make loving your neighbor a conscious daily practice. In a huge city, people come at you by the thousands. On the streets, there are so many that it bewilders you; and when you are crowded into subways or fast-moving buses or trains with so many others, it often seems insufferable. But Jesus Christ said that we should love one another. So if you and I want to live creatively and grow spiritually, we must practice loving people, not as groups of people, but individually, in Jesus' name. If each of us, loving ourselves as children of God and loving Jesus, would really begin loving all people as our neighbors, why, we would change the world in no time.

Without love, we are nothing. The Bible tells us:

> I may have all knowledge and understand all secrets; I may have all the faith needed to move mountains—but if I have no love, I am nothing. I may give away everything I have, and even give up my body to be burned—but if I have no love, this does me no good. Love is patient and kind; it is not jealous or conceited or proud; love is not ill-mannered or selfish or irritable;

love does not keep a record of wrongs; love is not happy with evil, but is happy with the truth. Love never gives up; and its faith, hope, and patience never fail. Love is eternal. (1 Corinthians 13:2–8, GNT)

One of the greatest skills in all the world, perhaps the supreme skill, is the art of loving people. In 1 Corinthians there is a stirring passage which concludes by saying: "Meanwhile these three remain: faith, hope, and love; and the greatest of these is

So faith, hope, love abide, these
three; but the greatest
of these is love.

1 CORINTHIANS 13:13 (RSV)

love" (1 Corinthians 13:13, GNT). To live effectively we must master the art of faith, we must master the skill of hope, and we must master the supreme genius of loving people.

A large part of our lives depends upon our relationship with other human beings. If we are in rapport and understanding and fellowship with them, life flows freely. If not, barriers are created which can be extremely unfortunate. What, then, is the status of your skill in loving other people?

Once, while in Pittsburgh, a number of people spoke of a distinguished friend of mine, Samuel M. Shoemaker, pastor of Calvary Episcopal Church of

Pittsburgh. He was one of the five greatest preachers of his time. I asked one man who had mentioned Sam Shoemaker with great affection, "Why are you so fond of him?"

"Because," the man replied, "he helped me find myself, a self I never knew I had. And," he added, "Sam is a great artist in loving people." What a tribute, "A great artist in loving people."

How does a person become a lover of other people? I point you to the words in 1 Corinthians, chapter 13, that I think of as guideposts. "Love is patient and kind." That is how the verse reads in the Revised Standard Version. The King James Version puts it:

"suffereth long, and is kind." What singing, melodious words those are! Love is patient; love is long-suffering; love is always kindly; love is philosophical; love is even urbane.

Urbanity—here is a wonderful concept.

What does urbanity mean? It means the absence of rigidity and nervous tension; inner calm; the willingness and capacity to wait and to hope and to believe and not to be excited or upset. Urbanity—I believe many of us would be better equipped for loving people if we could just develop a little urbanity.

Love suffereth long and is kind. Being patient, not getting upset, being philosophical, and being charitable will go a long way toward making you an artist in loving people.

There was a man who went around criticizing Robert E. Lee; he called him all kinds of names. One of Lee's friends, referring to this man, asked Lee, "What do you think of So-and-so?"

"I think he is a very fine gentleman," Lee replied.

"What!" the friend exclaimed. "Don't you know what he thinks about you?"

"You didn't ask me what he thought about me. You asked me what I thought about him." This is why Lee is considered by the North and the South alike one of the most spiritual men in the whole of

American history. He was above agitation, above snippiness, above ill will.

Love suffereth long and is kind. Only if you are patient and kindly enough to wait it out with faith when you are attacked or misunderstood, will you become an artist in loving people. We are so quick to get angry, offended, and bitter—to fly off the handle.

There was a newspaperman, a reporter, who on several occasions had said some strongly critical things about a certain prominent political figure. One day he secured an interview with this politician. The great man, being angry about the things the reporter had said, proceeded to give him a tongue-lashing, called him all kinds of names. The reporter just listened.

Because a person calls you names, that doesn't mean you are what the person calls you. He knew he was not what he was being called, so he just waited until the man ran down. Then the politician, in his angry mood, began to criticize other people, saying sharp, mean things about them. The reporter started writing these things down. He said, "Really, you are giving me a scoop. This is going to create a sensation. What do you think about So-and-so?" And again he wrote down what the man said. Then he asked, "These things you have said, do you mean them?"

Love is the only force
capable of transforming an enemy
into a friend.

MARTIN LUTHER KING

"Yes, sir, I mean them."

Then the reporter asked, "Will you initial my notes, because my editor is not going to believe they are right unless I have your initials."

"Yes, sir, I will." And he initialed the notes.

The reporter then folded the paper, tore it up into small bits and dropped it in the wastebasket. Astonished, the politician demanded, "What is the matter with you? Don't you want your notes?"

The reporter answered, "No, I don't like the things you have been saying. I have disagreed with you in the past, but I know you are a much bigger man than these mean, vindictive things you have said. I don't want the public to see you this way. So I have dropped it all in the wastebasket and have forgotten it."

By this time the great man was a great man again. He looked at the reporter and said to him, "Son, you are a very remarkable young man. You will go far in the world." And he did, too.

Which brings me to the final thing I want to say: "Love does not act unseemly." That too is from 1 Corinthians. There is a certain seemly quality about a Christian. Our function in life is not to create barriers but to eliminate barriers. Therefore Christian love has an essential, innate dignity about it. It does not conduct itself in an unseemly fashion. It is always spiritually strategic.

It is a great art, the art of loving people. Great is the happiness that comes when barriers are broken down and old hates cast aside, when old grudges are thrown away, and love enters in. So let us all so shape our attitudes and actions that we may live on that high plane of life where love never faileth.

A group of us stood on a hillside overlooking fields where occurred one of the greatest events in the history of mankind. In those fields, on a mystic and starlit night long ago, shepherds saw the heavens filled with a chorus of angels proclaiming peace on earth, goodwill to men.

I contemplated those fields, remembering that the shepherds, after viewing that angelic sight, said, "Let us now go even unto Bethlehem, and see this thing which is come to pass." And then our group, too, went to Bethlehem, a short distance away.

In that land, changes take place slowly. Camel trains are still silhouetted against the sky; people still ride little donkeys; shepherds still watch over their flocks by day and night, on rocky hillsides and in stony pastures.

At Bethlehem, our group lingered silently and thoughtfully at the place where Jesus was born. The land is honeycombed with the caves in which people then lived. Jesus probably wasn't born in a wooden stable as we know stables here, but in a cave where the animals were sheltered.

It is the same little town of Bethlehem over which the star stood, where the everlasting light proclaimed that here had taken place the greatest miracle of all.

A miracle is a wonder that we find difficult to explain. After we have learned to explain it, we no longer regard it as a miracle. One of these miracles is the miracle of love. Have you ever noticed the strange things that seem to happen to people at Christmastime? On Christmas Eve, for example, amid the throngs on the city streets, irritation is softened and stridencies become less. There is a flow of love, a community of understanding. Prejudice weakens and, for twenty-four hours, cities, towns and villages everywhere are different because people's hearts are different. I have never known this to fail, and I have often wondered why all of us could not be this way throughout the year. It is the miracle of love working magical transformations.

To love and be loved
is to feel the sun
from both sides.

DAVID VISCOTT

We must learn to utilize love as we have other powerful forces, such as heat, light, electricity, and mechanical energy. One way to do this is to express love freely. The more it exists within our thoughts, the more it will be expressed in the world as our action. Scientists have asserted that the reason humanity has survived upon this earth is because the total of love energy has thus far exceeded the total of destructive energy emanating from hate and revenge. Now that nuclear weapons and destructive powers have increased, we must compensate by expending more love energy.

When I began preaching, businesspeople and

scientists—indeed almost everyone—thought of love as something theoretical. Now, however, scientists and the so-called realistic thinkers tell us that the only practical way to live is by practicing love and goodwill.

I have always known that love really works. Years ago, on one of our early trips to Jerusalem, the Holy City, we saw people fighting one another. In the center of the city, there was an eight-hundred-foot stretch of desolation called No-Man's Land. On one side were warring Arabs; on the other, warring Jews. I was waiting at this No-Man's Land checkpoint to meet Father Patrick, a famous Franciscan priest. Finally, an old car chugging along was stopped by the sentry. Out of the car stepped a priest with a face that made you love him at once. Father Patrick was one of the best-known Christians in the Middle East. He could even cross the border unchallenged. At this meeting, the sentries gathered around him and he put his arm around them, saying, "Hi, boys! How are you all?"

I said to one of the sentries, "You fellows seem to love Father Patrick."

"Oh, yes, we all love him," he replied.

One of them waved an arm toward the other

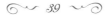

side. "They love him over there," he said, "just as we do here."

This Franciscan was going back and forth, weaving strands of love that no politician could weave, that no United Nations commissioners could bring about! It was a living demonstration that on those very roadways where Jesus walked, there was occurring a miracle of love. A modern disciple, Father Patrick demonstrated that people can learn to live together in goodwill.

We ought to stop thinking negatively about people and start thinking positively about the creative power available to each of us. Love that works between individuals will also work between nations.

Perhaps the idea of love working internationally in the relationships between peoples may surprise you. It should not. Have you ever actually, wholeheartedly, tried love instead of hate? When someone has done something that has annoyed or offended you, have you ever tried loving him into a good relationship, instead of fighting him back? Did you ever bless people for the mean things they have done to you? Have you ever overcome your prejudices and preconceived notions about people by learning to know and love them?

A man spoke to me once in a city where I was

scheduled to speak. I recognized him as the assistant to a seemingly very difficult executive in a midwest business. This assistant, "Bill," I will call him, had to report to his boss every day. "I would actually stand outside his door feeling cold all over," Bill told me. "My hands were clammy. I could feel chills going up and down my spine. And I knew he would either bark at me or receive me in stony silence. 'There, sir, there it is,' I would say, placing my report before him.

"He would look at it, then at me, and never say a word. Sometimes he would grumble, 'All right. Get going. I have it.'"

Of course this attitude stimulated a feeling of

Nor height, nor depth, nor any other creature, shall be able to separate us from the love of God, which is in Christ Jesus our Lord.

ROMANS 8:39

hatred within the assistant. He asked me what he ought to do. "Perhaps, if we were of the same faith, we might get together," he said.

"Well," I replied, "you are of the same faith in God. That makes you his brother. Have you brought the Bible to bear on the situation? I suggest that you try loving that man into a pleasant relationship."

"No one can love him," he protested. "There isn't a soul in the world who loves him."

"Then perhaps he is lonely and shy," I suggested, "and his spirit has retreated behind this domineering personality. Why don't you try an experiment? Pray for him, asking that you may understand him and be able to help him. Put tomorrow's meeting with him in God's hands. Think of this unhappy man and forget yourself, and when you stand outside his door in the morning, project thoughts of love toward him. Ask the Lord how you can help him."

Bill tried the experiment for a long time without results. Then, while they were discussing a problem in cost accounting, a subject in which Bill was an expert, they were bending over the desk, their heads close together. "Suddenly I felt a surge of love, like a wave of compassion sweeping over me," Bill told me later. "And when we had finished our discussion, the boss put his hand on my shoulder and said, 'Bill, I've come to depend upon you more and more. You mean a lot to me.' In that moment I saw, behind the stern exterior, the unhappy, lonely man you had suggested he might be."

Bill is no longer shrinking and inarticulate. "I want to tell you," he declared, "this power of love works. People I once disliked or looked down upon, I now appreciate and get along with."

That is what the baby born in a manger long ago came to tell us. I have often wondered about the wondrous power given Him at birth, which He exercised over human beings. Some mysterious quality was put into Jesus—into His smile, into His voice—

so that people, when they came close to Him, were changed completely. As they yielded themselves to Jesus, no matter what their weaknesses and failures had been, they were taken away. This is the greatest miracle of all—this "new birth" that takes place within human beings.

I don't know what your life struggle has been, what weakness, what sense of defeat, or what prejudice has plagued you. You know what they are. You may have struggled with them all your life, and been defeated by them. But the minute you yield yourself to the Spirit of Him who first came as a baby in a manger, you can be changed.

All over the world, people are singing about Jesus. What is the reason we love Him so? What is His power? It is the power of God who created us, and who is always re-creating us. Most unhappy people simply need the love and understanding of others who have the spiritual answer.

If you know what you are doing is wrong, if you feel weakness within yourself, or inability, just give yourself to Him and these things will fall away and you will be made new in Christ. That is why the shepherds said, "Let us now go even unto Bethlehem, and see this thing which is come to pass."

Miracles do happen, even today.